# Strawberries in November

# Strawberries in November

Mike Hanmer Walker

**To order additional copies of this book, contact:**
Xlibris
1-888-795-4274
www.Xlibris.com
Orders@Xlibris.com
663377

# CONTENTS

*In loving memory of*

*Mary Rose Walker*
*6th July 1931-28th November 2013*

# HALLOWEEN

**A**s the darkness falls, and the air becomes eerie and you have no place to hide,

your skin will creep, you will never sleep on

the night that the witches ride,

the night is scary, your soul is screaming its best to stay inside,

your lips will quiver, and your bones will shiver on the night that the witches ride.

your mind will go, you will lose control, your strength may soon subside.

you are under a spell, but no one can tell on the night that the witches ride,

fear for your life with slime on your walls and blood will cover your floors,

keep on running until the night is over and make sure that blood isn't yours,

beware of their powers, prepare to hide and keep yourself out of sight,

for it may be you who they are looking for..those witches who ride tonight.

# STRAWBERRIES IN NOVEMBER

**A**s the years go rolling by, and you know nothing stays the same,

just go along with the flow, don't put yourself out of the game.

Enjoy your strawberries in November, you can take as well as give,

there is so much you can offer and enjoy, there is still a life to live.

Don't just watch your young ones get on with it, prepare to play your part,

And they may appreciate you too, as your staying young at heart.

still keep that spirit going and that is something they will remember.

Then with the passing of time, they too will enjoy their Strawberries in November.

# THE TASK

O kay time to get up and get busy, I will get it done I feel determined today,

There is a task that has to be done, and I shall see it through every step of the way,

I will not slack, Slouch or settle and there will not be any time for fun.

No, I shall carry on and I will never stop until this task is finally done,

Even if it's a task I won't enjoy, and never really wanted to do,

I shall show strong will and discipline, and I am sure I will see it through,

So please don't Interrupt or disturb me as I carry out this task.

Just give me the time to complete the job, that's all that I will ask.

And never think that I will give in, as I promise that I will not.

Well what is this task that I will complete today, oh bugger I forgot

# A WOMAN IN NEED

**R**ita was a lady who was getting a bit of stress,

well I say a bit...when in fact she was in a fine old mess,

She told me soon she was going to end it all and that she has had enough,

I said steady on girl, things can't be that bad really, what are you thinking of love?,

so I went to see if I could help and talk her out of it, well I would certainly try my best,

this is where I put all my skills on counseling and talking to the test,

I called at her house, and the door was open, but she was not inside,

so where could she be I wondered, where on earth could she possibly hide,

then I noticed her garage door was left wide open, and I had this awful feeling,

there she was inside she never looked at me, while she was fixing a hook on the ceiling,

i called out what are you doing in here. she said stop, I have given up hope, but why I replied, what is wrong, it will get better what are you doing with that rope?

no stop don't do it, I cried as she put the rope round her neck, first I have something to say,

go on then she asked, what is it?, I hope this won't take all day,,

so I told her there's no need to suffer, and told her my life story, I thought she may want to hear.

then it seemed to happen her smile came back and her face was free from fear,

so I asked are you feeling better now, and happier with yourself Rita?

she never answered for a while, but I was confident I knew how to treat her,

no I am not happy yet, she said, but soon I think I will be fine,

as she took the rope from around her neck and tried to put it round mine.

# OH WHAT A DAY

**W**oke up in the morning, and the heating has broke down and its cold,

and these things begin to affect you when you are

getting old,

never mind tea or coffee now which one shall I choose?

oh neither it would seem the kettle has blown a fuse.

let's see what's on TV then, oh no its gone berserk

the picture isn't there, the aerial doesn't work,

ok these things were sent to try us, I have always known,

well I would happily plead guilty if they left me alone,

so I will put my shoes on now, I don't really care.

oops my laces have snapped, and I don't have any spare.

what else can go wrong today, let's just wait and see,

I believe in god now, well someone's got it in for me,

it must just be one of those days, they happen now and then, that's ok but it would be good if I knew where and why and when.

at least I know there is something that is listening to me,

as I sat in my car and said "now don't you start" it took me literally,

I sat there thinking to myself now why is it all going wrong,

but I never really bothered to think too hard and long,

my mind was made up, I would not let it bother my head,

see you all tomorrow, I am going back to bed

# CHANGES IN ME

**A**s another day dawns on a brand new year, I sit here with quiet reflection,

And I notice changes in me year by year that create a new direction.

Changes in tastes and in opinions which I previously thought were set,

So what of the things I was so sure about, well I haven't made my mind up yet.

Well is it good to change direction, and look at things in a different light,

Maybe I won't accept these changes in any way. but then again I just might.

I used to love a pint or two of beer, and now somehow I can't stand the stuff.

So now whenever I go down to the pub for a drink, I am glad when I have had enough,

And that is how I think about these changes and how they may affect me personally

A tendency to analyze myself and my direction, but hey not to seriously

# THE PAST YEAR

**A** few things have happened in the past year, one of which I will always bless.

How my whole family became united in a show of togetherness.

I have made some new friends too, some I have come to trust.

And yet I will always keep my old friends too, (if I really must),

There have been highs and lows of course, that will happen come what may.

Yet even the tough times too I have learnt to face with a laugh along the way.

But some people have a different agenda to friendship so this is what I do.

If you offer me warmth and friendship, I will offer warmth and friendship too.

But if you are looking to exploit or take advantage, then you may be out of luck,

Because likewise if you just want to throw shit at me, then be prepared to duck.

# GETTING ON

**N**ow is the time to finally face the truth, those years have swiftly gone,

So I suppose I should slow down now, it's true I am getting on.

The fun days and the wild times are no longer, I must now commit them to memory,

I will remember those late nights with a naughty smile, but now its cocoa and slippers for me,

And no more misbehaving for me, from now on I will act like a saint.

The fun belongs to the young and lively, and young and lively I aint.

So shall I leave the partying to the young ones now, and sit here quiet and still.

just stick to these rules and watch the world go by...

Gigantic heck I will!

# BOOKS

I have a book on the paranormal, I never bought or found it in any way,

I just woke up in the morning and it appeared in my bedroom one day.

How to improve your memory, I know I have that book here too.

But I have forgotten where I put it down, I just haven't got a clue.

Now I have just had a tot of dark rum, and I think I fancy another,

Oh I forgot where I put that bottle too, because I hid it from my brother.

"How to avoid crime" was a book I went out shopping and picked.

But on the way home, you guessed it...I was mugged and had it nicked.

Well I thought I would write these things down just for a bit of fun.

I don't have much else to do at the moment, now where did I put that rum.

# DEREK AT 26

**D**erek at number 26 was a bit of character, a law unto himself.

He never gave much away, he never married, he was happy on the shelf.

If anything could possibly be used again Derek would always try.

When you walk past his garden you would see the teabags hanging out to dry,

One fine afternoon while sitting in his garden, well so the story goes,

A fly had landed in Derek's beer, which really did get up his nose.

He picked the fly out from his beer in anger, and then was heard to shout,

"I will pull your wings off you little pest, if you don't spit it out."

He then looked at the fly and without shouting, he would simply talk,

"Now listen if I pull your wings off, you won't be a fly no more, you'll just be a walk"

Well we have many different characters in our neighbourhood, we certainly have a mix.

But none of them quite as profound as Derek at number 26.

# MASTER OF THE REMOTE

L ets settle down and watch this film, I don't think I Have seen this one before,

No thanks I want to watch something else, I don't want to watch this film no more.

So pass me that remote right now, before I can sit here and settle,

This film is so old, I think it's been on more times than my grannies kettle.

What's this on the other side, oh its one of those competition things,

Where you are asked to vote on someone who dances, juggles or sings,

This looks like a cooking challenge, someone else who wants my vote.

This is so ridiculous, let's see what's on later, give me back that remote.

Don't make plans for later, I have already planned what to watch, I am sorry.

You will have to watch what you want somewhere else, cos tonight I'm watching Corrie.

Oh are you really, well I hope it doesn't last too long and finishes too late,

As I will be turning over if it does, because the football starts at 8.

Well we will see about that, now let's watch this side for a while,

Oh you must be joking, ok let's turn it over I am not watching Jeremy Kyle.

Hey why did you turn it over, don't you think I should have a say,

And by the way, who made you master of the remote control then anyway?

Does any of this sound familiar, Is it you, your partner, or your spouse,

Who takes control, and declares themselves Master of the remote in your house,

# IT'S SNOWING

It's snowing in the courtyard and the families are out in force,

The grownups complain about the cold, but they are loving it too of course,

Snowballs are flying everywhere, and no one is free from attack,

Oh no that one has hit him on the back of the head and some has gone down his back

I would have loved to join in the fun, but I am staying warm instead.

But watching from the window I can hear every word that is said,

No No! Caroline don't stick it there, Yes I can see he has no clothes,

but when you build a snowman, the carrot is meant for his Nose.

They will be out again tomorrow and continue with their play,

Well they may as well before it warms up and starts to melt away.

So the snow may be fun, but now you have had quite enough,

Until one day, someone finds some way of warming up the stuff

# A TRIBUTE TO.....

**I**ts a kind of magic who I am paying tribute to, can you guess the name?

come on friends will be friends and all you gotta do is play the game.

Don't stop me now, I am having a good time, in fact I'm having a ball,

And any way the wind blows doesn't really matter, Now I'm here I want it all.

Save Me I'm going slightly mad, but we are the champions I trust,

But if those fat bottomed girls would flash under pressure, then Another one bites the dust.

And I am just a good old fashioned lover boy and your my best friend I recall

It's a hard life but if you figured it out then we will rock you, it's a miracle

# LIKE STREET TALK

Is you listening man, but I mean like is you really listening doh?

Cos I is saying this is wicked, and I is thinking you should know,

I is really cool man, cos like I is learning quick.

I is doing this big time, and I is learning every trick,

Is you know what I is saying, or like don't you know a word,

Cos I is like want you to understand me, I is liking to be heard,

maybe you is still saying things like "oh lord" or "Gordon Bennet

but I is like not saying them no more, cos I is talking street talk ennit

# THE OWL AND THAT CAT

The owl and the pussycat went to sea in a beautiful pea green boat,

the boat capsized and the owl realised that pussy cats don't float.

Oh no said the duck, that is such rotten luck, I must go and see what can be done,

Swimming's a laugh said the cockney giraffe, but they don't seem to be having much fun,

Behind some trees was a lion on his knees, keeping an eye on events,

His wife too was there, but she could only but stare, as nothing was making much sense,

The duck had a thought, he swam out and bought an old abandoned raft,

but along came the beaver chewed the wood and would leave her, looking a little daft,

Let's all get on board, said the giraffe with a cord which tied the wood back together,

And it all held tight well into the night, but it wasn't going to last forever,

The fox was to blame as he was holding a flame which set the raft ablaze,

As the flames went higher the lion saw the fire and thought oh happy days,

He called over his wife who was holding a knife and said look what I have for you,

With this gift I will say happy Valentine's day, it's a big floating barbecue,

# A TOAST

**A** toast to those who have all they want, and a toast to those who have not.

To Those who don't have all they need, but cope with all they have got,

To those who are there when mistakes are made, yet don't hold their heads in shame,

But hold their hands above their heads and accept their share of the blame,

To Those of you who knows someone who has been lonely for a while,

And is ready to greet them as they pass by with a hello and a smile,

To Those who can offer a little help to those in need, with the little time they can afford,

And happily offer that little help without expectation of payment or reward,

To those who get it wrong, to those who get it right,

To those who say they will, To those who say they might,

To those who don't know if they can, and those who never ask why.

To those who have never done before, but are willing to give it a try,

To those of you who know so much, and those who really don't have a clue,

For while you are doing your best, whichever that may be,
Then here's a toast to you.

# A WEEK ON THE FARM

If you are from the city, and need a change for a while then spend a week on a farm,

I did it once and it was different and refreshing, well it certainly did me no harm.

The smell of the pigs and other animal's poo filling the air may not be a winner

But you will get used to it very quickly and it won't put you off your dinner.

and when the time comes to do some work, you may be asked to milk a cow,

but you may choose to stay where you are. by claiming you just don't know how,

I enjoyed my stay at that farmhouse. It was an experience to behold.

But alas I won't be asked back there again, i am afraid I have been told.

it was when I was watching from my bedroom window the horizon and the breaking of light.

Just enjoying that peace, so what happened next just didn't seem to be right,

A rooster was crowing loudly and proudly to welcome the brand new day,

So just for fun i picked up the farmers gun and just blew the noisy bugger away.

# THE TALES OF ARTHUR

D id you know there is life on Mars, its true Arthur once told me so

His uncle was an astronaut so he should somehow really know

Rats can be taught to how to talk, Arthurs cousin was a vet,

who told him so one day,

And the only reason you cannot hear them talking is because

they don't have much to say.

chicken pox and measles can be passed on by marine life or fishes if you like,

because Arthur knows a team of deep sea divers who were all infected by a pike,

so how do deep sea divers cope with all these diseases they can catch,

are deep sea divers with chickenpox really good enough? I mean do they come up to scratch?

oh smoking is not bad for you, it's ok to smoke as much as you really want to

Arthurs grandad smoked fifty a day, and he lived to one hundred and twenty two,

Now you may know someone like Arthur, and you may think he is a fool,

Just because he has a lot to say, and he talks a lot of bull.

# DORIS THE LADY

**D**oris was a model way back in her day, and wow she certainly turned your head,

She had a classic hourglass figure, and she would not only walk but give a wiggle instead.

And despite her advancing years, she still wanted to dress sensually with a view to please.

With a low cut top and heavy makeup and a dress that was a foot above her knees,

Doris does not think she is getting older and all those physical charms are no longer there,

She still believes she has what it takes to make the fellahs whistle, stop, and stare.

All the curves and shapes in all the right places, Doris still believes she has still got em.

Well she does still have that classic hourglass figure although

she now has 45 minutes at the bottom,

And Doris intends to enjoy her life whenever she can, and intends to have lots of fun,

because Doris knows and is very aware that tomorrow is not promised to anyone,

So go for it Doris go ahead and enjoy the rest of your life in any way you please,

Just don't give in, and keep that wiggle, that walk, that look.

oh you are such a tease!

# HAVE YOU EVER?

**H**ave you ever had one of those days that lasted more than a week,

When you just don't want to talk about it, because you just don't want to speak,

Or maybe you want to talk about it but there's always another fear.

You try to tell somebody but find that it seems nobody wants to hear,

So you just keep quiet about it, and each time you will always find,

If you don't speak or nobody listens, then it will always play on your mind,

Then you don't only want to talk about it, in fact you now want to shout,

"Hey can anybody hear me?" because I really need to work this thing out,

Well maybe there's one of many things, that you simply need to do,

Open your mouth to speak to someone but always keep your ears open too.

# KEEPING FIT

I was thinking now that I am getting on I had better start keeping fit and taking care,

So I started looking at the ads for gyms and exercise to find out when and where.

There are things like yoga, pilates and they ask if I can do press ups on my own,

Well that depends as the only press ups I do nowadays is the volume on my phone,

Ahh this one looks interesting it says how you can keep in shape absolutely free.

And anything that won't cost me any money has always been fine by me.

It read "over 50's keep fit for nothing" well I was thinking what a nice little touch,

But I am already fit for nothing so I won't be needing that thank you very much,

I think I will just be self disciplined and eat some salad with my grub

And then I will do my exercise with a bit of effort and run down to the pub.

# A BEAUTIFUL EVENING

**W**e gathered at my sister's place on the 28<sup>th</sup> of November,

To light a candle for our mum and nan so that we would all remember.

We spoke of many memories of what she would do and say,

And what m.um would be feeling if she were looking down today,

Well as we had a family group hug, we laughed as well as cried,

For the love we had inside that room, she would feel a great sense of pride,

Then we sent up two chinese lanterns, high up in the evening sky.

Then looked up to thank and bless our mum and nan, and finally say goodbye,

She can rest in peace now, and I feel we can finally let her.

As we all came away from the evening feeling so much better,

So I would simply like to finish now, just by saying this,

It was a beautiful fulfilling evening, well done and thank you sis.

# LOUISE

**S**he delivers my dressings and makes sure they are never late,

And she will make sure my medication is always kept up to date,

The dressings need to be packed in bags and delivered to my door,

Where she will ask about my tablets, and whether I need some more,

As my pills are carefully arranged in dosage boxes which make them easier to dispense

And Louise will fill those boxes when I need them I hope I am making sense,

She would give me the dressings which she has neatly packed into bags,

And take my empty pill boxes for refilling (which apparently stink of fags,

Now Louise is a pharmacy assistant and putting aside any joking,

I really must make the effort to permanently give up smoking,

Oh and by the way Louise is also the wife of my best friend Jim,

Well there may have been a problem here, if I never mentioned him,

So I am taking this given opportunity to do what I wanted to do,

To say how much I appreciate your care and help, and thank you so much Lou.

# REBECCA

**W**hether she is shopping or in the park she will call me on the phone.

And ask me what I am doing, and tell me when she will be home.

She will be there when her nan and grandad come along to visit me.

Where she will run to me and give me a hug, because I I I am her Mick you see.

When she is out with her Nan and grandad she will tell them to be quick.

Hurry up and finish your shopping, I want to go and see my Mick.

And when I see her and she runs into my arms it feels good to be alive,

for she is Rebecca and I am her Mick, even though she is only five.